MW01689023

Back a Sister Up:

I Am Commanded to Prophesy!

by

Denise L. Folks, Ph.D.

DORRANCE
PUBLISHING CO
EST. 1920
PITTSBURGH, PENNSYLVANIA 15238

Unless otherwise indicated, all scripture quotations are taken from the Holy Bible: King James New International; Life Application Bible; King James Version.

Dorrance Publishing Co
585 Alpha Drive
Suite 103
Pittsburgh, PA 15238
Visit our website at *www.dorrancebookstore.com*

ISBN: 978-1-4809-4560-9
eISBN: 978-1-4809-4583-8

The hand of the Lord was upon me,
and carried me out in the spirit of the Lord,
and set me down in the midst of the valley which was full of bones,
and caused me to pass by them round about:
and, behold, there were very many in the open valley;
and, lo they were very dry.
And he said unto me, Son of man, can these bones live?
And I answered, O Lord God, thou knowest.
Again he said unto me, Prophesy upon these bones,
and say unto them, O ye dry bones, hear the word of the Lord.
Thus saith the Lord God unto these bones;
Behold, I will cause breath to enter into you, and ye shall live;
And I will lay sinews upon you, and will bring up flesh upon you,
and cover you with skin, and put breath in you, and ye shall live;
and ye shall know that I am the LORD.
So I prophesied as I was commanded...

Ezekiel 37: 1-7

Contents

To all of my sisters, daughters, granddaughters, and to all women who have a desire to help mold and shape "her" into the image of God through wisdom, power, love, and a sound mind:

To the "Fivefold Ministry": My prayer is that you will be able to use the contents of this book within your women's ministries to help instill greatness in the midst of trials, tribulations, and transformations in the lives of all women.

Acknowledgments

I thank my Lord and Savior Jesus Christ for commanding me to write this book.

I thank my mother for always seeing the best in me even when I did not see the best in myself.

I thank my daughters, granddaughters, goddaughters and sisters for trusting me and believing in me to pray for them and prophesy to them in Jesus Christ's name.

And, I thank my husband, Bishop Victore' M. Folks for his encouragement, support and love for me and all women in Christian ministry.

Foreword

"Women's problems cut across race and countries."

Buchi Emecheta, Novelist, 1944

"I know who I am. I am not perfect. I'm not the most beautiful woman in the world. But, I'm one of them."

Mary J. Blige

"A wise woman wishes to be no one's enemy; a wise woman refuses to be anyone's victim."

Maya Angelou

"I am an example of what is possible when girls from the very beginning of their lives are loved and nurtured by people around them. I was surrounded by extraordinary women in my life who taught me about quiet strength and dignity."

First Lady Michelle Obama

"Every time you smile at someone, it is an action of love, a gift to that person, a beautiful thing."

Mother Teresa

"It is a foolish woman who expects her husband to be to her that which only Jesus Christ Himself can be"

Ruth Bell Graham

"God is concerned and He's working it out for you."

Shirley Caesar

"Charm is deceitful and beauty is vain, But a woman who fears the Lord, she shall be praised."

Proverbs 31:30

"And when Jesus saw her, he called her to him, and said unto her, Woman thou art loosed from thine infirmity."

Luke 13:12

From the Desk of Prophetess Denise L. Folks, PhD.

Dear Sisters:

Thank you for reading *Back a Sister Up: I Am Commanded to Prophesy.*

I wrote this book to you out of love. When I think about who I am in Christ, I cannot help but to thank God for you. It is women like you who encourage me and strengthen me to press forth to the "mark of the higher calling in Jesus Christ."

My love, commitment, and loyalty to Jesus Christ keeps me from wavering in my love, commitment, and loyalty to you. I'm moved with joy when I hear about your victories and accomplishments. You are a woman of distinction. Thank you for understanding your commitment to be who God called you to be. It's your uniqueness that attracts God.

Sisters, I am convinced that we must stay on the battlefield for the sole purpose of standing in the gap for one another in all seasons (spring, summer, autumn, and winter). I refuse to allow Satan to oppress, depress, suppress or impede the anointing that flows from me to you and from you to me which gives us freedom to express who God called us to be.

As I close, there is one thing that I must encourage you to do: Please believe that God called women to preach the Gospel of Jesus Christ. He has no respect of person. He has given women visions, prophecies, and dreams. Let no man despise her call. Support women in the ministry. Pray for them. Satan doesn't want women in the pulpit, and too many women feel the same way. Help pave the way for other women. Don't become selfish, nasty, jealous, envious, bitter or religious. We need her.

So, my sisters, stay strong in the Lord and be determined to "Back a Sister Up." You are commanded to Prophesy!

God Bless You Forever,
Denise L. Folks, Ph.D.

Let Me Hear Your War Cry!

There's a roaring deep within; a crying in my soul
Screaming, Mercy! Mercy! Mercy! Birth pains I can't control
Curled up in a fetal position, my spirit in a knot
What is this thing that's rumbling? What is this cry about?
Lift up your voice you warrior. The Lord spoke to me
From every mountain and valley, set the captives free
Let me hear your war cry! Sound it loud and clear
The power I birthed inside you, release without fear
Open the mighty flood gates, till the fallow ground
Receive the wounded soldiers; Affirm, Confirm, Astound!
Let me hear your war cry! Be the head not the tail
Let me hear your war cry! In Christ you cannot fail
Prophesy my daughter! Speak to the Valley of Dry Bones
Prophesy with Power! Give hope to their weary moans
Scream, holler, shout; Mountain Get Out of My Way!
I'm marching into ~~to~~ power. My war cry is to pray
God, save every nation, Mend their broken heart
Open the prison doors, Let your spirit impart
Let Me Hear Your War Cry! North, South, East, West
Let Me Hear Your War Cry! Be mighty in your quest

Introduction

The purpose of this message is to challenge you to look beyond your own circumstances and see her: your sister, daughter, mother, grandmother, girlfriend, next door neighbor, coworker, stranger, and even your enemy.

There are many women in the Bible who I can write about:

The woman at the well, the woman with the issue of blood, Mary Magdalene, Naomi, Ruth, Hannah, Tamar, Queen Esther, Sarah and even Mary, Jesus' mother. These women found themselves in the midst of rape, homelessness, hunger, envy and jealousy, pregnancy, disrespect, adultery, fornication, murder, shame, sickness and betrayal. These are just a few of the soul- wrenching catastrophes that ushered them in to the presence of an almighty God. But I will not share their stories.

In the proceeding pages, I will tell you about women who you see every day. You don't have to journey back through the Old Testament or the New Testament. They are in your midst every day. I will share their stories. And I will explain some of the reasons for their conditions and how you can back them up by prophesying to them. You may be one of them. You may know one of them. As you read about their trials, tribulations, transformations, and victories, pray for them. Some of them are the Valley of Dry Bones. We must prophesy life.

The Valley of Dry Bones refers to Israel's spiritual deadness which resulted from their kingdom being divided after the death of King Solomon. The division caused a condition of hopelessness and doubt to filtrate and settle in their spirits. God used Ezekiel to speak life into their situation. He commanded Ezekiel to prophesy to the people. As a result of Ezekiel's obedience to God and his belief in God's word, the dry bones came to life. Hope was restored. The kingdom of Israel was once again standing to its feet like a vast army ready to live again (Ezekiel 37:1-14)

Let us prophesy truth so that our sisters, daughters, mothers, grandmothers, girlfriends, neighbors, coworkers, strangers, and yes, even our enemies can be restored in Jesus Christ and live again.

Women are Commanded to Prophesy

Joel 2:28 and Acts 2:17-18 state, This is what I will do in the last days, God says: I will pour out my spirit on all flesh: your sons and daughters will proclaim my message: your old men will have dreams and your young men will see visions. At that time I will pour out my spirit even on servants, both men and women.

God called and commanded women to speak life into the lives of others. As women, we have an awesome responsibility to see into the conditions of our sisters and speak those things that are not as if they were (Romans 4:17).

God desires that we be cleansed and renewed in our hearts by His spirit in order to be able to prophesy to the Valley of Dry Bones (Psalm 51:10-14).

Hearts and attitudes must be right with God and united with one another so that we can touch and agree with our sisters in the name of Jesus Christ (Matthew 18:19).

God is at work calling His people back to Him. He wants us restored in body, soul and spirit (Colossians 1:20).

You must receive the baptism of the Holy Spirit to prophesy to God's people. The word of God states that, "Ye who are spiritual restore such a one back to fellowship" (Galatians 6:1).

As women, we must:

1. Come up and out of our dead states.
2. Prophesy to our own condition.
3. Denounce the past and be delivered.
4. Prophesy truth to other women.
5. Be in love, committed, and loyal to Jesus Christ.
6. Have faith that Jesus is at work in your life and her life.

The Lord Shall Reign

Forever, Your God,

O Zion, to all

Generations.

Praise the Lord!

Psalm 146:10

"If You Allow God to
Reign Fully In You,
God Will Rain On You
and Over You
So You can Reign
With Him."

Come Here

I heard the voice of someone beckoning me to "come here"
I heard the voice of someone commanding me to draw near

The voice didn't sound strange I've heard it times before
There was no doubt in my mind It was the Lord for sure

I heard the voice of someone beckoning me to "come here"
I heard the voice of someone commanding me to draw near

The words were so profound like thunder in my soul
He spoke from heaven to me My name was on his roll

I ceased from doing something and quickened my mundane pace
I had to get to Jesus to fall upon my face

As I entered into His courts the atmosphere was so sweet
I lifted my hands to praise Him And bowed to kiss His feet

The angels started singing the song was just for me
I started shouting- Thank you, Lord!
My soul at last was free

I heard the voice of someone beckoning me to "come here"
I heard the voice of someone commanding me to draw near

As God's word drew me closer my darkness turned to light
In the midst of my misery I began to regain my sight

As joy filled my temple, God whispered in my ear
"You are my daughter, Woman"
"Have faith. No need to fear"

I heard the voice of someone beckoning me to "come here"
I heard the voice of someone commanding me to draw near

I was the woman at the well
No longer will I thirst
He's filled me with His water
He's redeemed me from the curse

I touched the hem of His garment in humble submission on my knees
Just a little touch of Jesus healed my blood disease

I heard the voice of someone beckoning to "come here"
I heard the voice of someone commanding me to draw near

And when he putteth forth His own sheep, he goeth before them, and the sheep follow Him: for they know His voice. And a stranger will they not follow, but will flee from him; for they know not the voice of strangers (John 10: 4-5).

My sheep hear my voice, and I know them, and they follow me: And I give unto them eternal life; and they shall never perish, neither shall any man pluck them out of my hand. My Father, which gave them me, is greater than all: and no man is able to pluck them out of my Father's hand. I and my Father are one (John 10:27-30).

Urgency

I have an urgency to meet God
I have expectations of his might
Nothing is going to stop me
I must attain higher height

Zaechaus climbed the sycamore tree
The woman with the issue of blood
The man lowered through the roof
A blind man's sight restored with mud

His awesome, magnificent, power
Seeps deep within my soul
Rejuvenating my inner man
The Holy Ghost taking full control

I'm climbing Jacob's ladder
Gonna stay on the narrow path
No time to deal with nonsense
Rebuking all malice and wrath

I am saturated by his presence
Engulfed from above
Wrapped in his mercy
Captivated by his love

I have an urgency to meet God
I'm destined to break through
I have an urgency to meet God
This breakthrough is for me and you

God's word is the truth
So mountain – ! Get Out of My Way!
I'm on a special assignment
Somebody - Help me pray!

My opponent tried to strike me out
Sickness, bitterness and pain
But I'm fighting the good fight of righteousness
Through the lightning, thunder and rain

I'll run this race with vigor
Victory is in the air
I'm sliding in to home plate
Praise God, I'm almost there

I have an urgency to meet God
I have expectations of his might
Nothing is going to stop me
I must attain higher height

"But ye are a chosen generation, a royal priesthood, an holy nation, a peculiar people: that ye should shew forth the praises of him who hath called you out of darkness into the marvelous light"

1 Peter 2:9

"You Need Power

And Passion

To Walk In Your

Purpose

To Receive Your

Promise"

Drowning Royalty

Main Scripture – 1Peter 2:9: "But, ye are a chosen generation, a royal priesthood, a holy nation, a peculiar people: that ye should shew forth the praises of him who hath called you out of darkness into His marvelous light."

Royalty means superior. It pertains to a kingship, magnanimous, magnificent, stately, a person of rank, noble. It is grace and peace abundantly through the knowledge of God. It's relationship with Jesus Christ, and knowing Him in the pardon of your sins.

Put on Your 'Life Savior'

Drowning Royalty is a term I use to describe sisters who don't know who they are in Jesus Christ. And, because of this, she doesn't know what her purpose is. Without purpose, she has no authority or power. Drowning Royalty is characterized by cluelessness in which direction to take. This sister takes every fork in the road; she jumps on every band wagon; she jumps to every preached message. Basically, she lacks the ability to be attentive. She believes that she can sustain herself without the buoyancy of the word of God. She attempts to tread in the deep waters of life without her 'Life Savior.' As she starts to drown, the enemy takes advantage of her desperation, ignorance of God's word and her inability to hear from God. He quickly and strategically makes his move by surrounding her with sharks, who like sheep in wolves clothing, nip away at her body, soul and spirit. Fake girlfriends, illicit lovers, unsaved family members, and back-sliding friends sublimely whisper in her ear, "You'll never be anything; no one loves you; you are fat and ugly; you will be alone the rest of your life; you can't preach; you missed your calling; you're going to die!"

This sister is drowning because she made the fatal decision not to establish a relationship with her 'Life Savior' – Jesus Christ. She's under a serious spiritual attack from the devil. She looks like a drowning victim; she's doing everything she can do to be rescued by somebody, anybody. Her butt and breasts are exposed; her eyelashes and hair are all in her face and her mouth is wide open, not to mention her legs. Her attempt to be rescued is futile. She needs a powerful sister in Jesus Christ to rescue her. She doubts that she can ever attain to royalty in Jesus Christ so she desperately and breathtakingly reaches for whatever edge she can. Her doubts cause her to drown in self-pity believing herself to be a victim and not a victor.

Question: Are you a Life Guard who can lead her to the 'Life Savior'?

Jesus Christ is our Life Savior. He uses his Shepherd's Hook/staff to draw us closer to him for an intimate relationship, to inspect us and to keep us from wandering in what we think is greener pastures. He does this because we are his sheep and he cares for us.

It's Time to Come Forth and be Healed

The woman with the issue of blood – Come Forth!
The woman caught in adultery – Come Forth!
The woman in prison – Come Forth!
The abused woman – Come Forth!
The woman with no job to feed her family – Come Forth!
All those afflicted with sickness and disease – come forth.
Murderers, thieves, prostitutes – Come Forth!

Receive your healing. Embrace it. Let nothing or no one rob you of it.
You must open your mouth and proclaim your healing.

Open Your Big Mouth and Proclaim Your Healing
Prophesy to your condition. Let Me Hear Your War Cry!

It's like rivers of living water in your belly. Pull down strong holds and vain imaginations. We wrestle not against flesh and blood but against spiritual wickedness in high places; against principalities; against the rulers of darkness. You have the power and authority through Jesus Christ to speak life! Prophesy to your condition. Speak to the Valley of Dry Bones! Death and life is in the power of your tongue.

SCREAM, HOLLER, SHOUT!
THE LORD HAS GIVEN ME THE VICTORY!

Lie Prostrate Before Him

Now, lie on your face and give honor where honor is due. Make love to God. Tell Him that He is everything to you. No more tears of pain and disappointment. Oh, taste and see that the Lord is good. He's sweeter than the honey and the honey cone. He's your creator. Worship Him! Cry sweet tears of joy. Humble yourself.

Revelation 3:20-22: "Behold, I stand at the door and knock: if any man hears my voice, and opens the door, I will come in to him and will sup with him, and he with me. To him that over-cometh will I grant to sit with me in my throne, even as I also overcame, and set down with my Father in His throne." He that hath an ear let him hear what the spirit saith unto the churches.

Stand to Your Feet Woman of God!

Take off your shoes for you are standing on Holy ground. Only the pure in heart shall see God. Ask God to search you, know you and try you to see if there is any wicked way in you and lead you in the way everlasting (Psalms 139:23-24).

Matthew 28:19-20

You have received your assignment. Go ye therefore, and teach all nations, baptizing them in the name of the Father, the son, and the Holy Ghost: Teaching them to observe all things whatsoever I have commanded you: and, lo, I am with you always, even unto the end of the world.

In Conclusion

We can never sit idly by allowing the enemy to steal, kill and destroy who God called us to be. We are Royalty. God said it in 1Peter 2:9 – "But, ye are a chosen generation, a royal priesthood, a holy nation, a peculiar people; that you should shew forth the praises of Him who hath called you out of darkness into His marvelous light." The enemy is here. He is roaming the earth like a roaring lion seeking whom he may devour. We must watch as well as pray for one another. We are our sister's keeper. You are commanded to Prophesy! We bind and rebuke the spirit of Drowning Royalty and proclaim our Kingdom Position and Purpose!

Naomi

Naomi, Naomi, Naomi

Don't hide your face from me
I need your knowledge, wisdom, and embracing arms
Don't you hear my heartening plead? ...

Naomi, Naomi, Naomi

I have pains deep within
I've been battered by a world infested with the stench of sin...

It may seem as though I'm rebellious
Or refuse to see the light
That paves the road to virtuousness
Godly dressing, speaking and walking right...

You may not understand my jewelry or makeup
Or wonder why my nails are so long
I may not to jumping and shouting with the Holy Ghost
but my spirit has a longing song...

It sings, teach me, guide me, love me
Don't ignore the forest for the trees
Don't give up on me Naomi. Tell me!
How do I obtain those righteous Kingdom keys?...

I am a young woman filled with energy and zeal
I want to put it in the master's hand
So my life in Him can be real...

Naomi! Naomi!

Don't you hear my youthful cry?
Come from behind the walls of Christendom
Help save a young woman.
Don't let her die...

The world, my flesh and Satan I wrestle with night and day
Hold me. Rock me. Love me. Don't let my soul decay...

I'm calling on you Naomi
I'm that voice in the wilderness
I thirst for your knowledge and wisdom
To behold, cherish and caress...

In Jesus' name, lead me down the path
paved in diamonds, rubies and gold
I know there will be some potholes
as I'm transformed to the new forgetting the old...

Please remember, if I seem uninterested
or cute to take spiritual, godly advice
Have mercy! Have mercy! Pray harder!
Don't you think I'm worth Calvary's price?...

Young women, God has sent us a Naomi
Don't ignore what she has to say
Be receptive to her teachings
Learn from her wisdom and godly way...

Naomi! Naomi!

Thank you, Jesus!
She has come to help build my house
Cooking, cleaning, womanhood
And, how to take care of my spouse...

Naomi!

You are so special
You have so much to give
Hold me. Rock me. Love me.
In Jesus' name your guiding light encourages me to live...

Look at Me!

Look at me!

I'm beautiful. I'm Proud
I'm God's Woman

I see you looking out of the side of your eye

Look at me!

Acknowledge me
No need to make pretend that you don't see me

I see you looking, It's okay
Watch me

I'm Beautiful. I'm Proud
I'm God's Woman

I think so and so do you

You think I'm on some vanity trip
You think that I think I'm cute
Well, your perception is erroneous

Look at me!

You don't know what I had to go through to feel like this

So, look at me!!
See pass my outward beauty
See my soul
Feel my Power!

I've overcome the stench of this messed up world
I've survived some of my darkest days
I've passed many hard trials and tribulations

It was God who told me to stand strong
It was God who saw my pain
It was God who tasted my tears

So, look at me!
I'm Beautiful. I'm Proud
I'm God's Woman

Look AT ME!

I was motivated to write this poem after observing a young woman who appeared to be in her late teens or early twenties. She was walking in downtown Baltimore. She walked proud and determined. She seemed to know who she was and what she was to become. Her youthful features were not despised by drugs, alcohol or a Jezebel demeanor. In her eyes I could see a tenacity that was probably birthed through hard trials and tribulations that were sent by the enemy to destroy and kill her destiny. Abuse, neglect, and abandonment once pierced her tender heart. Yet, she struggled and fought off many attacks with no help from those who promised to protect her. As she maneuvers through the busy city, she knows that the world sees her; hates her; admires her. She is a survivor. She didn't die at the hands of the world, her flesh or Satan. God kept her in the midst of it all. She welcomes the world to look but don't touch.

A Portrait of Self-Esteem

I believe that some women cannot 'Back a Sister Up' because she is within herself empty. The struggle to find out who she really is may be frightening. She has been everything to everybody yet never taking the time to nourish who God called her to be.

Every time she makes an attempt to feel good about herself, she's reminded of her physical and emotional challenges that are a result of childbearing, a struggling relationship, or poor self-image. This is exacerbated by financial and educational road blocks.

As she wrestles with the world, Satan and her flesh, seemingly to no avail, she starts to believe the lie that the enemy keeps screaming in her ear, "You are dumb and worthless!" As she tries to rise up to fight for her God-given destiny, she grows tired. Weakened by the enemy's constant blows at her head and heart, and gut, she simply gives up and collapses.

This feeling of discouragement brings on an "I don't care" attitude. She believes yet another lie: "Nobody cares about me." With this self-loathing spirit, she begins to treat other people in the manner in which she feels. Lying, bleeding, and dying on the Jericho Road, she has no strength to get up and live for herself, not to mention others. The enemy has come to kill, steal, and destroy.

A woman struggling with any infirmity can be healed and delivered by touching the hem of Jesus' garment. But, she must surround herself with women who know who they are in Christ and who have a desire to get her to the Savior.

The problem with this woman is she surrounded herself with women who were discontent within themselves because they had no relationship with Jesus Christ. They were unable to offer her a sincere helping hand or an attentive ear. They could only offer her bitter advice and fruitless 'messtimonies.' She eventually collapsed in their presence. They did not have the power of praise and worship in their belly to resuscitate and rescue her. She was left for dead by the hands of the enemy, and by those she mistakenly confided in.

In summary, her feeling of discouragement made her jealous and envious of those who could help her. She despised the commitment, conviction, and compassion of other women. She saw herself small and feeble in their eyesight. This is another lie that the enemy told her. When looking into the mirror of her soul, she didn't see hope and love; she saw helplessness and despair. She saw herself eternally bound to her condition. Her darkness was great.

Moon Dancing in the Darkness of a Lie

The sun descends beyond the infinite wonders of heaven's sky. The consciousness of light is slowly fading.

I tell myself over and over again, "Not tonight. I refuse to be swallowed by the darkness of a lie."

Turning away from the window, my image speaks to me, beckoning me to look closer; "Mirror, Mirror on the wall, who's the fairest of them all."

My features have changed, not gracefully but disgracefully. I've allowed the winter days of life to ride in on the wings of my youth before its time.

Not giving into pity or shame, I convince myself that this is my last dance, my last romance with darkness.

Tonight, someone will see me, notice me, and want me to love me. No longer will I have to 'Moon Dance in the darkness of a lie.'

The curtains of a brand new night open. The familiar smell, taste and sounds of night sensitize my flesh sending quivers through my dimly lit soul.

My soul is given the cue, "Action, Action." My appearance transforms to fulfill my 'Moon Dance' role.

I step quietly into the moving silhouette of the dimly lit sky. Someone sees me, notices me, and wants me to love me!" I disappear into the darkness of a lie once again, praying that this is my last `Moon Dance,' my finale, my last cry in 'The Darkness of a Lie.'

The aged women likewise,
that they be in behavior
as becometh holiness,
not false accusers,
not given too much wine,
teachers of good things;
That they teach the young
women to be sober,
to love their husbands,
to love their children, to be discreet,
chaste, keepers at home, good,
obedient to their husbands,
that the word of God be not blasphemed.

Titus 2:3-5

Women in Their Rightful Position

Mature Christian women must be in their place in the home, church, and community in order to keep Satan off of their daughters. They must have a strong relationship with Jesus Christ. Satan desires to rape and molest little girls and young women of their dignity and self-worth. Without a strong relationship with Christ, older and, supposedly, mature women in Christ will not be able to spiritually wage war on the adversary.

Yes, young girls and younger women are in full bloom. They are in the spring of their lives. They do think that they are "all of that and a bag of chips." But this does not give the enemy the right to attack them. It does not give us the right to put them down by calling them names, rolling our eyes at them, and refusing to mentor them due to our own jealousies and insecurities. We can't dislike them because our man keeps peeping at them. Don't you know that our sexual sins have visited our daughters and granddaughters? We cannot stand back and watch them go through what we went through. They may not be as fortunate as we were to escape and survive beatings, rapes, molestations, abortions, substance abuse, incarceration, foster care, and outright abandonment. Therefore, we got to go into Satan's kingdom and wage war. We must put on the full armor of God in order to tear his kingdom down. The spirit of Sodom and Gomorrah will not replicate it's evil and seductive ways in the lives of the women God called us to protect.

Satan and his cohorts are harsh and shrewd. They have no respect of person. They wait outside of the womb for our daughters to put into full effect the fatal blow. The word of God says "we are born in sin and shaped in iniquity." The forces of evil start planting seeds that will rob them of their destiny while our daughters are in the womb. Illicit musical lyrics, television shows, negative people and negative conversations speak death to the unborn fetus which can feel and hear everything. Alcohol and drugs ingested by the pregnant woman adds insult to the unborn child's spiritual injury. Our young girls and women have no idea of the damage that they may be causing. If we, as mature Christian women, look back on our own young lives, some of us were no better. But we can change that by speaking life over them and not death, and by living a life pleasing to our heavenly Father.

Women, if we are not whole within ourselves through Jesus Christ, we can only cause our daughters more injury.

Women, let us get in our "Rightful Position" in Jesus Christ. We need each other.

Woman to Woman

Woman to Woman
I thought you had my back
Woman to Woman
What a vicious heart attack

I opened my life to you
So tired of standing alone
A sister in the making
To help endure my burdens, my groan

But you couldn't see pass self
It was all about your pain
You couldn't even press to touch
His garment for another's Holy Ghost rain

Back a Sister Up!
Is my constant cry
Don't cripple her with maliciousness
For her well will soon run dry

Ruth and Naomi
Martha and Mary too
Both had their differences
But to each other they were true

Woman to Woman
I thought you had my back
Woman to Woman
What a vicious heart attack

You came upon me like a thief to kill, steal and destroy
I was blinded by your words and deeds
Your strategy of decoy

I looked for a woman to stand in the gap
As I fought for our right to be heard
I looked for a woman to stand in the gap
For bold preaching of God's Word

The essence of true sisterhood is no secret to unfold
The essence of true sisterhood
Agape love, Now that's bold

I know you didn't mean it
You're a child of the most high God
Your emotions held you captive
And made your heart grow hard

I'm not holding it against you
The pressure must have been great
Why else would you tell others
That I speak words of hate

Silly women do things like that
Laden with great sin
You've been washed with the Blood of Jesus
His love now abides within

Don't ever do what you did
It will come back one hundred fold
You'll find yourself running through the woods
Without shelter from the cold

Woman to Woman
I'm really praying for you
Please help "Back a Sister Up!"
Bring her face to face with Jesus

It's her time to sup

Judas Iscariot is dead
The Pharisees are no more
The Body of Christ, The Rock of Ages
Like the wings of an angel I'll soar!

I'm not coming down off of the wall
To deal with the world's lie
I'm a warrior in Jesus army
For tis not my time to die!

Almost wounded in the house of a friend
Thank God, I ducked in time
I've grown stronger in the process
Up Zion's mountain I must climb

On ward march you soldier!
I hear the Master cry
Pick up your up your cross I'm calling
Prophesy truth. Don't Lie

Your battle wounds are minor
Now watch as well as pray
Turn down your plate and listen
I'll steer you in my way

The enemy is raging
Goats and wolves in sheep's clothes
My sheep will hear my voice when calling
And won't retreat to angry woes

Lift up your voice in Zion
Speak to the "Valley of Dry Bones"
Ignore the madness of others
Sooth their weary moans

Woman to Woman

Please try to understand
I am more than a girlfriend
I was called by God to lead and guide
Standing steadfast from beginning to end

Girlfriends come and go
Tell you things you want to hear
But a true friend sticks closer than a brother
In Jesus, she calms your fear

She will tell you things you don't want to hear
And push you strong and hard
She will pierce the heavens with her prayers
For you to get to God

She will even block Satan's nasty blows
And catch you when you fall
She will encourage you to go forward in your divine call

Therefore

When you think of me
Be careful what you scream
I'm covered by the Master's Blood
In Him I am Redeemed

Sincerely,
Your Sister

Every wise woman builds her household, but a foolish woman tears it down with her own hands

Proverbs 14:1

Your hurt and bitterness can run so deep that it tears into the very fabric of another sister's soul

Nasty A.S.S. Women
(Another Silly Sister)

This topic has been written especially for you. It is not to be used to critic your friend, sister, coworkers, the girl next door, the prostitute, or your baby's daddy girlfriend or wife. It was written so that we, as women, can take a good hard look at ourselves for the purpose of changing all aspects of our being to wholeheartedly meet the needs of other women internally and externally.

The hurt and bitterness that some women have experienced can be embedded so deeply in their souls that it causes them to strike out and tear into the very fabric of another sister's soul. It can even cause her to speak curses over men and children. We must begin to use our spiritual insight to explore and, when necessary, tear down strongholds and vain imaginations that keep us from being a blessing as opposed to a curse in the lives of other women.

Nasty A.S.S. (Another Silly Sister) Women is a terminology that I've chosen to use to describe some of us or most of us depending on our state of body, soul, and spirit at a particular time in our lives. Some may be offended by this term. I can only ask that you put your feelings and judgmental opinions aside for a minute until you have examined the contents of this topic.

The American Heritage College Dictionary, Third Edition, defines "nasty" as being disgustingly dirty; physically repellent; morally offensive; indecent; malicious; spiteful; very unpleasant or annoying; painful or dangerous; grave; exasperatingly difficult to solve or handle; bad.

The King James Bible defines "nasty" as immoral; filthy; indecent; wicked; violent; jealous; angry; ambitious; envious; drunkard; fornicators; idolaters; adulterers; disgraceful; and obscene; all that is contrary to purity; dirt; defilement; lasciviousness; wantonness; disregard for decency; greedy; contentious;

shameful; foul; cruel; unjust; undisciplined; spoiled; wasteful; rebellious; unchaste (Galatians 5:19-21).

The American Heritage College Dictionary, Third Edition, defines "ass" as vain; silly; or aggressively stupid person. The same reference describes "asshole" as a thoroughly contemptible, detestable person.

The King James Bible refers to an "ass" as one that is washed going back to wallowing in the mud (2 Peter 2:20-22).

The definitions and scriptures stated supports and bears witness to the topic:

Nasty A.S.S. Women, better known as Another Silly Sister.

This sister really needs a lot of prayer. How did she get to be so nasty and silly?

Proverbs 31, virtuous woman, list attributes of a woman that are seemingly unattainable for the woman of today. She cooks; she cleans; she sews; she's an entrepreneur; she handles the finances correctly as she budgets for the winter; and most of all, she brings great honor and pleasure to her husband and children to the point that they call her blessed.

Who is this woman? Has anybody seen her? She is the woman at the local Department of Social Services trying to get money for her children. She is the woman at the laundromat with six bags of clothes to wash and dry while the king stays home fast asleep. She is the woman on the bus stop at 5:30 a.m. with her baby on the way to the day care center and then off to work or school. She is the woman at the clinic with the child infected with HIV passed on by her long-gone lover. Can I get any more specific? All of this and more may have reduced her to a Nasty A.S.S. Woman. I ain't one to talk but, her baby daddy girlfriend said, "She ain't nothing but a bitch with a funky attitude on a bad hair day."

I beg to differ. This woman was you and me trying to make things work out with somebody we thought loved us. We would have done anything to make the right love connection. We are wired like that. God put the desire in a woman to be covered by a man spiritually, emotionally, and physically, but the covering just wasn't there. You got hooked up with somebody who had no idea of how to cover his penis let alone cover a woman. He had no relationship with Christ; therefore, he had no true relationship with you. Now that you are convinced that it is not working out, you try your luck with the next man. "All right," you say to yourself, "this one goes to church. I'm on the right road now. He can sing, shout, pray, and do the Holy Ghost dance. He can even preach a little bit. Watch out! Y'all, I'm gonna be a First Lady!"

Wait a minute. He's always too tired to have Bible study with you. You rarely see him reading his Bible outside of church. He hangs out with people who are not spiritual. He doesn't want to talk about marriage. He's content with the way the relationship is going – living together, spending your hard-earned money, and hanging out with the boys. You're right back where you left off in the last relationship. Your life has become a vicious cycle.

As a result of all the preceding circumstances, bitterness has taken up residence in your heart. Let's not forget the responsibilities that your biological father failed to fulfill in your life. You're just one messed up sister. Low self-esteem has planted its roots in you. Now he has a new girl. Your body may have lost its youthfulness due to child bearing that brings on additional weight and stretch marks. You start to verbally and, in some cases, physically attack him or the other woman. The other woman is on the rebound too. She doesn't know your plight with him. She's just trying to fill a gap in her heart the same as you. But now she just became "Another Silly Sister" in the life of another sister.

My question to you is: Do you want to be delivered? Do you want to be made whole? Do you want to "Back a Sister Up"? If your answer is yes, read on. If your answer is no, quickly pass this message on to another sister. You are either deeply hurt or bitter and have allowed your circumstances to cripple you. Or, you don't think that it's your responsibility to bring healing and deliverance to someone else. Maybe you just haven't grown to this level of spirituality yet. I pray that you will someday.

Warning! There is one thing that you must understand. And that is, some women have no desire to change. They don't want to be a blessing. They take pleasure in being Nasty "A.S.S (Another Silly Sister) Women." The word of God says that they are "silly, sin-burdened women." Women of that kind are forever following new teachers, but they never understand the truth. They allow themselves to be seduced by those who have dirty, warped and twisted minds who have turned against the Christian faith (2 Tim. 3:6-7, Life Application-Living Bible).

What to Do When Other Women are Nasty to You

Just because she acts nasty doesn't give you the right to be nasty to her.

Check it out. When another female acts nasty to you, smile. Most of the time, it's best not to say anything. A silent prayer and Christ-like behavior may allow you to minister to her at a later date.

While you are taking a spiritual inventory of her, try not to be misled by her hair, nails, clothes, car, man, children, or detestable habits or idiosyncrasies she may have.

Like the woman with the issue of blood, she too must press through to receive her healing and deliverance. If we fail to introduce Jesus Christ to her through our actions, verbally and non-verbally, we become a stumbling block to her.

How Do I Avoid "Another Silly Sister"?

You can't avoid "Nasty A.S.S. Women." They will be here until the end of time. Jesus Christ said, "Be in the world but not of the world." If you are studying and meditating on the word of God, they will avoid you. Darkness and light has no fellowship. If you keep finding yourself in her company, ask God to search you, try you and know you to see if there be any wicked way in you and lead you in the way everlasting (Psalm 139:28).

Make sure that you are not living a compromising lifestyle. If carnal-minded and unsaved people sense compromise in you, they will not avoid you. On the contrary, they will be drawn to you.

How Can I Guard Myself from Becoming a "Nasty A.S.S. Woman?"

The only surety in guarding yourself from being labeled as such is to stay in God's presence. The word of God teaches us in 1John 1:7 "But if we walk in the light, as he is in the light, we have fellowship one with another, and the blood of Jesus Christ his son cleanseth us from all sin."

Hoochie Coochie Mamas

Hoochie Coochie Mamas in all colors, shapes, and styles
Hoochie Coochie Mamas with sexy, crazy, sneaky smiles
Hoochie Coochie Mamas wearing splits up to her thighs
Hoochie Coochie Mamas with craving, hungry, starving eyes
Her talking and her walking has a certain kind of spark
You see her in the morning, in the noon day, in the dark
It's your mother. It's your sister. It's your daughter, cousin, and friend.
It's your grannie. It's your auntie. It's your teacher. Is there no end?
She turns the heads of children and other women looked cock-eyed
Men are who she's seeking to really boost her pride
She's a female acting crazy, unwise, a foolish girl
Being virtuous is a mystery. She has no time to be a pearl
She loves to be noticed, played with by human eyes
She's flirtatious in her dressing to protrude her luscious lies
She kinda throws it all together, something cheap that gives a peep
Then sashays through your marriage, your church – this Mamas' deep
She's a Hoochie Coochie Mama on a mission with a plan
You better get your house in order beit woman or man
She's a Jezebel-Delilah sweet nothings dripping from her lips
She's a Jezebel-Delilah spreading sin with her hips
You better get your house in order for she's heading straight your way
You better get your house in order. If she enters, she will stay
For she's a Hoochie Coochie Mama in all colors, shapes, and styles
She's one of Satan's angels come to sift you with her sexy, crazy, sneaky smiles

Diaper County

Black sister think she's making it
Taking it
Shaking it
Exposing, posing
Giving up what's chosen
Spreading luscious lies
Big brown thighs
Daddy lies, dies
Baby cries
Government check
Thinks she's fly

"Awake Thou That Sleepest, And Arise From The Dead, And Christ Shall Give Thee Light."

Ephesians 5:14

Get Up!

It's Time to go

Straighten Up!

Position of Greatness

Stay Up!

It's Your Destiny

Rise Up! Rise Up! O Bride of Christ

Rise Up! Rise Up! to the house of the Lord.
Today is your day.
You have been chosen to sit at His feet and sup at His table.
You have been chosen to be His Bride, the Bride of Jesus Christ.
Open your heart. Open your mind. Open your spirit.
Receive your blessing.
Jesus has ordained this day to pour you out a blessing,
a blessing that you have not room enough to receive.
Prepare yourself as His righteous Bride.
Adorn yourself with precious thoughts and deeds.
He is coming for you, His Bride, His church without spot or wrinkle.
Will you be prepared?
Rise Up! Rise Up!
No more self-pity, shame, depression, abuse, sickness, slothfulness, calamity!
Take the challenge! Embrace the good fight!
Show the world, and Satan that Jesus is your everything!
He is your healer, deliverer, your light, your life!
Will you rise up and show the world His glory?
Will you allow Him to dwell richly in you?
Will you stand firm on His word telling your sisters, brothers, friends
and yes, strangers about His everlasting Love?
Yes. Today is your day. You are His Bride. You are His Queen.
You are virtuous.
You are God's Changing Woman.
You are flesh of His flesh and bone of His bone.
Rise Up! Rise Up! O Bride of Christ.
Prepare yourself for the Bridegroom.
He is coming. He is coming soon.

Song of Solomon 2:10-13
My beloved spoke and said to me;
Rise up, my love, my fair one, And come away!

For lo, the winter is past. The rain is over and gone.
The flowers appear on the earth; The time of singing has come,
and the voice of the turtledove is heard in our land.
The fig tree puts forth her green figs, and the vines with tender grapes
give a good smell.
Rise up, my love, my fair one, And come away!

Sleeping Beauty, Please Wake Up!

You've heard the old fairy tale about Sleeping Beauty. If not, let me refresh your memory. At the time of her birth, an ugly old witch cast a spell on a baby girl. Once she grew into her teenage years, death would strike, causing her to fall into a deep sleep never to wake again. Well, with each year, the child grew more beautiful than the year before. Everyone around her forgot about the spell that the witch cast on her when she was a baby. But the witch did not forget. The very day that the girl became a teenager, the witch put her plan in to action. She tricked her into touching a deadly sewing needle laden with poison. The beautiful teenager immediately fell into a deep sleep. She slept for years until a kingly man kissed her and broke the spell. At last, she was no longer in darkness, dead to the fulfillment of life. She gave her life to the kingly man and lived like a queen in his mansion for the rest of her life.

Question
Are you a Sleeping Beauty?

In order to answer the above question, you must ask yourself: What is a "Sleeping Beauty?"

Well, the story tells us that this beautiful young girl slept for 100 years because of the curse that was spoken over her life. No one that she surrounded herself with attempted to try to break the curse. Therefore, she remained dead to her surroundings. The fairy tale talks about a physical death. And it is just that, a fairy tale.

The "Sleeping Beauty" that is being presented to you is not a fairy tale young girl sleeping on a bed of flowers to be some day magically awakened with a kiss from Prince Charming. This sister is "phat" to death with track that's all that! She wears the latest clothes, knows all the latest songs, and all of her friends got cars. Her cell phone rings all of the time. You see, she's all that! She's so fine that God needs an appointment to talk to her. He tried to call her several times but, she said, "Hold on God" and then had the nerve to forget to click her phone over. This "Sleeping Beauty" is sleep walking or better known as the "walking dead." Everything about her is tied up in her looks. Vanity has reared its ugly head. The devil has taken full control of all of her senses. Her state of sleep is so deep that you can see the yellow crust in the corners of her eyes that keeps her blinded to the truth.

Her parents and other love ones try to cover her with the word of God and prayers, but she seems to think that she knows everything. Satan has taken full control of her mind. She actually believes that her parents are against her. She has traded them in for unsaved friends who have not retained God in their conscience. They can't even pray for her. They have crafted a plan to strip her of her covering that will leave her barren and destitute. Yet, she still refuses to believe that Christ is the way, the truth and the life (John 14:6).

Daughters, Do You Want the Truth?

The fear of the Lord is the beginning of knowledge; but fools despise wisdom and instruction (Proverbs 1:7).

Let no man deceive you with vain words; for because of these things cometh the wrath of God upon the children of disobedience (Ephesians 5:6).

The thief cometh not, but to steal, and to kill, and to destroy; but I. have come to give life and that more abundantly (John 10:10).

Present your body a living sacrifice, holy, acceptable unto God, which is your reasonable service. And be not conformed to this world: but be ye transformed by the renewing of your mind, that ye may prove what is that good, and acceptable, and perfect, will of God (Romans 12:1-2).

Remember now thy creator in the days of thy youth, while the evil days come not, nor the years draw nigh, when thou shalt say, I have no pleasure in them (Ecclesiastes 12:1).

My little children, these things write I unto you, that ye sin not. And if any man sin, we have an advocate with the father, Jesus Christ the righteous (1John 2:1).

My Dear Daughters

God looks at the heart of a person and not the outward appearance. God is all spirit therefore we must worship Him in spirit and in truth. Your looks will fade one day. You must understand that you may have a sleeping disorder that needs immediate attention. If so, Sleeping Beauty, PLEASE WAKE UP! Jesus is knocking at the door of your heart. Don't you hear Him? You have to let Him in. He has to know that He is welcomed. He wants to kiss you gently on your forehead and wake you up. He desires to break the curse that has been cast on you. He is the great healer and deliverer.

WAKE UP! WAKE UP! WAKE UP! Time is running out. The ugly witch is on her way back with seven witches more deadly than she is. They don't want you to wake up. Satan wants you bound to him. He doesn't want you brought from darkness into the light. He wants you blinded to your flesh, the world and him. Can't you feel Satan's stronghold holding you down with pride, vanity, disobedience, drugs, sex, bitterness, jealousy, confusion and lies? Come on "Sleeping Beauty," repeat after me:

Lord Jesus, please save me from myself, Satan, and the world. I believe that you are the son of God and that you died for me on the cross. I know that I am a sinner. Come into my heart right now to guide me in the paths of righteousness. Amen.

Romans 10:13 states, "For whosoever shall call upon the name of the Lord, shall be saved."

Burning Questions from Daughters

Q. If there is a burning desire to become a "Sleeping Beauty," why can't I become one and just be aware of my surroundings?

A. Daughter, you belong to God. He formed you in your mother's womb for his good pleasing. God desires for you to be blessed and not cursed. When you plan to be a Sleeping Beauty, you plan to go Satan's way. It is impossible for you to watch your surroundings every minute of the day. God has dispersed angels to do that for you but your desire must be for Him. He desires to keep you from all seen and unseen danger. Satan sets up traps for you to fall in. In order for you to be a Sleeping Beauty, you must step into Satan's Kingdom and give him free course to your life. To be a Sleeping Beauty you become deaf and dumb to the things of God. It's like having on a blindfold. You don't know which way to go. You become confused. Once Satan has you all messed up, thinking that you're all that, he comes in for the kill.

What's the kill? I'm glad you asked: Drugs, AIDS/HIV, abusive relationships, unwanted pregnancies, failing grades that lead to dropping out of school, shattered dreams, incarceration, emotional trauma, psychological problems, homelessness, helplessness, hopelessness, loneliness, and the list goes on and on. Satan's desire is to strip you of all of the power and authority that you have a right to in Jesus Christ.

Choose today who you will serve. Do you want rewards or curses? God gives us a free will. It's all up to you. You must exhibit the fruit of the spirit which is love, joy, peace, patience, kindness, goodness, faithfulness, gentleness, and self-control (Galatians 5:22-25).

Q. How many times do you have to have sex to get pregnant?
A. It only takes one time. I was fourteen years old when I got pregnant. It was my very first time.

Q. What signs should a person look for if they are pregnant?
A. The signs of pregnancy are different for each person. The first sign is usually a missed period followed by nausea or the desire to sleep a lot. If you think that you are pregnant, you should see a doctor as soon as possible. You can also go to see the school nurse.

Q. Why do boys make you feel the way you feel?
A. I don't know what feeling you are talking about, but I do know that God created boys and girls to be attracted to one another. Remember to always put Jesus first. He will lead and guide you in your feelings. Jesus said, "I am the way, the truth and the life: no man cometh unto the Father but by me" (John 14:6).

Q. Why do certain girls have sex just to get a disease?
A. I don't think that certain girls believe that they can get a disease. Some people ignore the information that is given to them that will help them avoid diseases. They believe that it's something that happens to other people. Hosea 4:16 says, "My people are destroyed from a lack of knowledge; because you have rejected knowledge, I will also reject you."

Q. How old do you have to be to have sex?
A. The Bible teaches that your body belongs to God and that you must present it to him as a living sacrifice, holy and pleasing to Him. This is your spiritual act of worship (Romans 12:1-2). Therefore, you should ask God to help you

stay a virgin until you are ready for marriage. Let Him prepare you for the man that he desires for you to marry. That is the day that God allows you to have sex. If you have sex before that time, you may mess up your chances of marrying the man God is preparing for you. Do not allow foolish girlfriends or horny boys to talk you out of your blessing. Once you lose your virginity, it is lost forever. I believe that most mature women in Christ will tell you that they wished they had waited. I know that I do. Ask God to "keep you" until that time comes. Let no one despise your youthfulness and purity.

Q. What happens to your self-worth once you have premarital sex?
A. Having sex before you are married, whether you are a youth or an adult, can create a bond with a person that God did not intend for you to marry or be with. This bond can bring you into curses that the other person has attached to his life (financially, socially, emotionally, and spiritually). When a male penetrates a female for the first time, he breaks her hymen, which is a thin sheet of skin that covers the entrance into her cervix where sperm is deposited. The blood from the hymen spills onto his penis and covers it. This begins a spiritual connection with that person that can affect you for the rest of your life even once the relationship is over physically. This spiritual connection or covenant relationship can also affect future relationships. This can happen with every person that you sleep with. God may not have had in His plans or thoughts for you to enter into covenant with that person. Jeremiah 29:11 states, "For I know the thoughts/plans that I think toward you, thoughts of peace, and not of evil, to give you an expected end." Your first covenant relationship should be with Jesus Christ. Remember, God's ways are not your ways. When you choose to have sex before you are married, you violate and disregard the word of God by choosing to satisfy your flesh. Satan uses your flesh to enter into your presence. Once you allow him in through fornication or adultery (sex with someone who is not your husband or wife), you set off a chain reaction that can result in unwanted pregnancies that often lead to abortions.. The relationship may not last or may turn out to be very detrimental to you. All of this will affect you emotionally and spiritually causing you to believe that you are worthless. Eventually you will start to seek love from others to try to ease the hurt that you feel.

Stand firm on keeping yourself for the Lord. The devil wants to kill, steal, and destroy you before you meet the man who God has already chosen for you.

Jesus comes to give you the abundant life. You are worth waiting for.
Dare to be different.

Adelphi

My sister called one day and wanted to give her life to the Lord
The life she had been living held no hope for the divine reward
Satan tried to stop me. I wasn't sensitive to her at all
I just couldn't believe that she was answering the holy call
He set it up so smoothly; dressed in a disguise;
He sent his demons to oppress me putting blinders on my eyes
I couldn't feel her pain or hear her dying plead
My heart was cold and hardened rejecting her long-awaited need
Satan's plot was against me. He thought he had me on the run
But I called for my heavenly father for protection through His son
My heart started to melt as we both shed tears
She surrendered her life to the Lord after so many unsaved years
The anointing was upon her as she lay lamenting to the Lord
I'll pray that she endures forever seeking God's heavenly divine reward

Adelphi is a Greek word which means "siblings." It is used of natural relationships. Matthew 19:29 speaks about being able to leave natural brothers, sisters, mother, and father for Christ's sake. Matthew 13:56 speaks of Jesus' natural sisters who were birthed after the Virgin Birth of Christ. Matthew 12:50 describes sister as of spiritual kinship with Christ, an affinity marked by the fulfillment of the will of the Father. Jesus states, "for whoever does the will of my Father in Heaven are my brother and sister and mother."

In conclusion, God calls us to be sisters in Christ and to bear one another's burdens.. Whether it is a natural or spiritual sister, we must always be reminded to back her up with the love of Christ. We must not leave her bleeding and dying on the Jericho road.

A Cry for You

I cried for you deep in the night deep down within my soul...
Pain forced its way up through my heart; My joy and strength it stole...
I thought I had you figured out; brave, strong, young and wise...
You mislead with your empty words while teasing with your eyes...
Roaming, seeking desperately those whom you may devour...
Weaving webs of deception; killing softly all who bow...
I pray for all your victims and those you seek to trap...
I ask that you have pity when you strap them to your lap...
They are somebody's daughter and son that you deceive...
Where is your grace and mercy? Cry out to Jesus if you still believe...
Oh yes! I still love you but God loves you even more...
It's not too late to turn to him; your soul He desires to restore...
He'll make a way out of no way. Do you really want to stop? ...
He'll send angels to surround you slaying demons until they drop...
I can't fight your battle or claim the victory's won...
It's your prayers to the Father that will seal your fate through His son...
So stop thinking about yourself and saying, "It's all about me."
Consider other people.
Stop spreading HIV....

The Road You Chose

Aimlessly planting life seeds of pain and strife
When will you stop, turn around, pick up the pieces, tears of a clown?
The road you travel is dimly lit
There is no flicker, death dwelling pit
I called to you, Watch Out! Watch Out! You ignored the call
And shouted
"I must see what it's all about."
I labor in prayer, standing in the gap, discerning your madness, foolish trap
I fall to my knees, head bow, eyes closed, watching and listening, your sorrow-
ful woes
Run for cover!
Hide under the sheet!
The enemy is roaring, a soul to eat
Run!
It's not too late
The Father's bosom, salvation's gate
No time to fear.No time to cry. Must escape quickly. No time to die
Grab my hand
Hold on tight
Stay close to me
I am the Lord
Choose your road
Damnation or Reward?

"Be sober, be vigilant; because your adversary the devil, as a roaring lion, walketh about, seeking whom he may devour."

1 Peter 5:8

"Move deliberately and strategically towards your ordained destiny"

Name Your Enemy

1 Peter 5:8

Be sober, be vigilant; because your adversary the devil, as a roaring lion, walketh about, seeking whom he may devour.
Never waste your time or energy fighting people.
You really have only one major enemy in life... Satan.
He simply walks around "as a roaring lion."
Jesus is The Lion of Judah. Satan is no match for Him.
It is Not Dangerous to Have an Enemy.
It is only dangerous not to identify him, her, and it.

Scriptures: Job 1:7; Proverbs 28:15; Matthew 24: 42; Mark 4:15; 2Tim. 4:17; James 4:7; Peter 1:13; Rev. 12:10

Vocabulary:
Vigilant: watch; we should exercise careful circumspection as one does when he is in danger. We are to be on our guard against the wiles and powers of the evil one.

Adversary: one that contends with, opposes, contest, resists, enemy, Satan, the devil, an opponent

Devour: to engulf; to swallow up; to prey upon; to eat up greedily; To destroy; consume destructively; waste; devour

Let Me Expose Satan

I was sleep not one time but on several occasions when I felt that old lust demon rise up to attack me. I tried to break loose but couldn't. I tried to call my husband for help but that demon had a hold of me. When I finally broke loose with the power of the Blood of Jesus, I felt raped; taken advantage of. All I could do was lie in the bed and weep. My husband asked me what was wrong. I could not even explain it to him. I laid there for a long time feeling wounded, helpless and fragile. Yes. This was a spiritual attack. My spirit was raped and molested. Satan tried to make me feel violated and weak. He does not want me to go forth in my ministry call.

Let me assure you that this is true. This attack actually happened. Now, if Satan can attempt to cripple me so that I can't go forward in the power that is rightfully mine through Jesus Christ, what do you think he is doing to our daughters and granddaughters who may not be aware of their power in Jesus Christ? How are we to protect them and prophesy over them in the midst of this shrewd and bitter adversary?

After praying about the attack and seeking God's wisdom and instruction, I rose up with greater power and determination in an effort to expose the enemy for who he, it, she really was. I started informing others about his tactics of sexual attacks.

If we are not careful about the type of people we let in our homes; the people we associate with; the places we visit; and, the things we allow in our ear-gate and eyesight through television, music and today's technology, we inadvertently invite Satan into our children's bedrooms. Many times our children are sexually promiscuous because of a demonic attack. Yes. That's right. Their first sexual encounter could be with a demonic spirit. They won't say anything because they believe it to be a dream. The attack is real.

As Godly women, we must never cease to pray throughout our homes, churches, and communities. We must walk in and out of our children's bedrooms and pray. Pray over them while they are sleep. You may be rebuking and binding a sex demon.

Therefore, the Bible says, "Be sober; be vigilant; because your adversary the devil, as a roaring lion, walked about seeking whom he may devour" (1Peter 5:8).

That Old Devil Laughed at Me

I was praying like a warrior
Trying to get to God to see
When I heard a nasty chuckle
That old devil laughed at me
My body started shaking
And sickness filled me up
In fear
I stopped in the midst of praying
Left with an empty cup
Nobody there to help me
I thought I was standing all alone
when my spirit started groaning
And my prayer turned to a moan
Articulation distorted
My tongue moved more and more
The words that filled the atmosphere
Came from heaven, that's for sure!
I was praying like a warrior
Trying to get to God to see
That old devil stopped his laughing
God's spirit fought for me!

The Fire Within

I was mad as a hatter for what I thought was serious matter
I rolled my eyes and stomped my feet
For what I thought was shear deceit...
I lost all composure and started shouting loud...
I put wrath in the atmosphere piercing heaven's cloud...
God in all His Holy Power spoke mercy in my path...
Hush, listen, my daughter
"Be quick to hear, slow to speak and slow to wrath...

Don't let your anger keep you from seeing, entering and possessing your Promise Land.

This poem is based on the book of Numbers 20:1-13, which details Moses' anger and what it cost him.

Dumber Than I Thought

I have a new friend in my life. He is everything that I have been looking for in a relationship. He is patient, kind, loving, and forgiving. I feel good about myself when he is around. I feel like a new person. Life has become more bearable and promising. I want to be with him all of the time. I have finally found my soulmate.

One morning, right after spending a beautiful evening with my friend, I woke up feeling weak and shameful. I couldn't understand what was going on. I tried to figure out what all the dread was about. Every time I tried to lift my spirit I heard a lot of noise and sensed chaos in the atmosphere. I tried to call my new friend but for some reason I could not get an answer. As I turned to reach for a book that my new friend had given me that was filled with promises for a greater life, I heard a knock at the door. When I opened the door my old friends, 'Dumber Than I Thought,' Lust, Deceitfulness, Vanity, and Pride walked right in.

They started reminiscing about the good old days and how much fun we used to have. I just sat and listened. For some reason, I couldn't remember how much fun it used to be. My new friend filled my mind with new thoughts which made me feel good about myself. My past seemed so futile and empty.

'Dumber Than I Thought' started getting mad at me. He said that I was a traitor and that I thought that I was "all of that" since I started hanging out with my new friend. I listened to his accusations. He also accused me of only hanging with my new friend because of what He could do for me.

'Dumber Than I Thought' said that he noticed that I walked and talked different. He asked, "what happened to the limp in your walk and the slur in your speech." He said, "Your walk and your talk use to be crooked but now you stand taller and speak stronger. Is that a sparkle in your eye?" And, "what's that light around you?"

Lust, Deceitfulness, Vanity, and Pride started easing away from me but 'Dumber Than I Thought' shouted in a loud and death screeching voice, "Get back here!" As they hurried back to his side, he motioned to them to surround me.

Lust jumped in my face and filled my eyes with hot sex images that tantalized my flesh with desire. Pride whispered in my ear, "Go ahead give in to it; you deserve to feel good; you work hard doing for everyone else; it's time you get yours." Vanity lured me to the mirror showing me my outward beauty and unappreciative passion. Deceitfulness told me that I needed to have a secret lover to fulfill and satisfy my sizzling flesh that was being neglected by my new friend. He said, "Go ahead, he'll never know."

'Dumber Than I Thought' took me to a high place and showed me all that I was missing by hanging out with my new friend; the late-night parties with the best liquor and drugs; the trips to gambling casinos and lude and lascivious music and movies; and the finest clothes and jewelry that would make a blind man regain his sight.

My flesh began to weaken. How sweet it all sounded. Just as I was about to take that fatal leap back into my past, I remembered my friend telling me that, "No man who puts his hands to the plow and turns back is fit for the kingdom." (Luke 9:62). . I quickly repositioned myself for help by dropping to my knees and praying. I cried out to God asking Him to deliver me from Satan, my flesh, and the world.

'Dumber Than I Thought' and his friends started laughing hysterically at me. They were laughing so hard that they were holding their stomachs and crying. This only made me pray even harder. But it seemed like the harder I prayed the weaker I felt and the louder and harder they laughed. The images that they filled my mind with were peering at me while I was praying. Why won't they just go away?

Vanity kept laughing and telling the others how stupid I looked kneeling down and crying out to the Lord. Pride whispered, as he always does, "Get up. You don't have to beg no body for nothing." Lust and Deceitfulness just kept peering at me from the corner of their crazy, sexy eyes. And 'Dumber Than I Thought' stood there laughing and commanding them to continue suppressing me.

Where was my new friend when I needed Him? He was a friend that stuck to me closer than a brother; He told me that he would never leave me nor forsake me; He said that he was my burden bearer. I repositioned myself again by lying face down on the floor. And, with every fiber of my being I called on him for help! I opened my big mouth and shouted, "The Blood of Jesus is against you Satan!"

All of a sudden, my natural tongue turned to a moan. I began to utter a language that even I didn't understand. Let me explain:

I was praying like a warrior
Trying to get to God to see
When I heard a nasty chuckle
That old devil laughed at me
My body started shaking
And sickness filled me up
In fear
I stopped in the midst of praying
Left with an empty cup
Nobody there to help me
I thought I was standing all alone
When my spirit started groaning
And my prayer turned to a moan
Articulation distorted
My tongue moved more and more
The words that filled the atmosphere
Came from heaven, that's for sure
I was praying like a warrior
Trying to get to God to see
That old devil stopped his laughing
God's spirit fought for me

I never felt so much power in my life. I could not see my new friend but I could feel him so strongly standing right beside me. My spirit man was instantly catapulted to another dimension; the third heaven where God resides. 'Dumber Than I Thought' started looking at me in a strange way. He began to back away from me lowering his eyes and bowing his head to the ground as if he was bowing to me. Lust, Deceitfulness, Pride and Vanity ran behind him in fear, shouting, "Leave us alone! Leave us alone!"

The atmosphere in the room changed from darkness to light. The powerful force of God that illuminated the room caused the forces of hell to be expelled.

‘Dumber That I Thought’ fled from my presence with his friends running behind him. As he was leaving, he looked back and said, “I’m not finished with you.

My new friend whispered in my ear, “Continue to draw nigh to God and the enemy will flee.”

Yeah, ‘Dumber Than I Thought’, Lust, Deceitfulness, Pride and Vanity were some of my closest friends for a long time. I stayed weak, pitiful, and broke while I was hanging with them. But my new friend, Jesus Christ, showed me a better way of life. He showed me a life that was more productive and spiritually uplifting.

My old friends really thought that their attack on me was going to draw me back into my old ways. They were ‘Dumber Than I Thought.’ They only made me see them for who they really were – robbers, killers, and destroyers. My new friend came into my life so that I could have life and have it more abundantly. I give Him all the Glory!

Don’t let the enemy of your flesh, the world, and Satan suppress, oppress, or depress you and make you fearful, weak, and shameful. If you have accepted Jesus Christ in your life as your personal Lord and Savior, be confident that he has forgiven you of your sins and desires that you walk in the newness of life with him.

Let your testimony be, “Satan and his cohorts are ‘Dumber Than I Thought.”

The End

Don't Be Caught by the Witch

Watch out before it gets you
It's coming straight your way
Those ugly little some things
To make you curse not pray
It comes in all forms,
Colors, shapes and sizes
It will grab you in the collar
Until you scream and holler
It will make you lose your cool
Speaking words of discontent
Forsaking the many blessings
That holding your peace has sent
The witch wants to hold you
Rocking you in her arms
Tearing down your blessings
Brick by brick with words that harm
Don't be caught by the witch
She comes in a disguise
Silly women in your bedroom
Spewing rumors, malicious lies
The enemy is out to get you
The goal- to take you down
To the pit – a dirty dungeon
To be molested, gagged and bound
Wake up you're not dreaming
This stuff is quite real
It comes to destroy and kill
Your soul it wants to steal
Don't be caught by the witch
Ignore her crafty way
If you listen, she will trick you
What a terrible price to pay

Run, Talk to Jesus
Let Him ease your troubled mind
Transform your thoughts to heaven
You're no longer deaf, dumb, and blind

"For nothing will be impossible with God."

Luke 1:37

"Your life has
meaning in your
valley of Despair; the
twisting and turning
of your pain sculpts
your capacity to bear"

Wrath on the Brink of Spring

How could he beat her like that? They were lovers. They were inseparable. They were in the world and the world was in them. Passion and lust had seemingly found a place in their hearts.

As the excitement and freshness of their new love gave way to fading novelty, secrets were exposed.

On a bright spring day, after the gray of winter had subsided, lovers became enemies. Inseparable became separable. The world that they were so much a part of had over taken them. Passion and lust had betrayed them.

In wrath, he pounded his fist into her face and body. From a distance, I could hear her screaming and crying. Their endangered relationship that seemed promising and blissful before was now satisfying the jealousy and envy of those who relished in its demise. Curiosity peered through the windows of houses, cars and businesses. People stood motionless, idly doing nothing. They appeared to be turned on, mesmerized, and engulfed in what was supposed to be a desperate cry for help.

This scene had permeated my mind over and over again as I revisited my own time of painful passion and lust that once had me caught in the same world of bondage. Are these the same people who stared and watched as I was being pounded and desperately crying and screaming for help? I often wondered, what would happen if I saw someone else being over taken by such wrath? What would I do?

I had grown to hate the mere thought of being talked to any kind of way. If I was pushed, shoved, or hit, I would fight to the death. I was willing to die for my right to be a woman of substance. I was a woman determined to be free of any preconceived restraints or constraints of a controlling and domineering spirit.

Fear had no longer gripped my very soul. Anger had taken root against the self-centeredness, ill will, and emotional frailties of the male ego which needed to be stroked, bowed to, and pampered. I was not going to be coveted or converted. I belonged to God. I was His property.

As the pounding, screaming and crying filled the atmosphere, I moved closer to the scene. I was able to see into her spirit, her soul, and her need. Embarrassment was able to find a place amongst her relentless sadness and pain which was evident by her attempt to hide beneath the shadow of an old oak tree. As the crowd grew, her pride tried to fight back. She exclaimed, "I'm gonna kill you, mother fucker!" and then threw an exhausted punch. This only made her situation appear more destined and detestable.

I pitied her. Yet, at the same time, I hated her. How could she allow this to happen? Where was her strength; her nobility; her virtue; her passion and determination to stand firm and ward off this roaring and raging beast whose passion and determination was to rob her of her youthful beauty; steal her love and joy for life; and kill her chances of ever being elevated to her rightful position as a queen by any man?

My flesh cried out, "Fight, girl! Kick him where it hurts! Bust him upside the head! Fight to the death! Please!" My soul became desperate. "Bite, scratch, growl. Don't curl up and die! Don't go out like that! He can be defeated."

My spirit started praying, but the attack was so disturbing that my natural man took flight to fight. I must stand in the gap. Scenes from my past flooded my mind. I couldn't wait for the God who delivered me to deliver her. What if she never called on God? What if she didn't want deliverance? I couldn't take any chances of her staying in that situation. How embarrassing. How weak. What if other women started acting the same way?

When I should have been interceding, my flesh moved closer to interfere. I must set the captive free. Adrenaline rushed like blood through my mind and soul. No time to master my emotions. Wrath gripped me in the pit of my stomach. How could I be motionless, idle at a time like this? I must act NOW!

I reached into my jacket. I pulled out the gun. I pointed it. And I pulled the trigger! BANG! BANG! BANG!

The pounding stopped. Screaming and crying ceased. Tears dried up. Sirens rang out. The crowd faded. All pain was gone.

Freedom had arrived on the brink of spring. And yet, the roaring, raging beast still roams the earth seeking whom he may devour.

Man That's My Daughter!

Man, that's my daughter that you're trying to get at
That's my little dear one so don't you dare say, "Damn! She's phat!
Yea, I saw you looking trying to get a peek
I saw your tongue hanging out of your mouth
You're so dumb and weak...
You can't have any daughters
that you protect from ravenous wolves and thieves
You can't be a young girl's brother or daddy
That she cleaves to and believes...
Let her grow up at least until she's twenty-one
Don't put your hands on her virginity
Stop tainting her purity
Stop destroying her youthful fun...
Out of all the women in the world
You allow your mind to be fixed on a child, a teen...
Attacking her in the prime of her life
Spinning a web to destroy a future queen...
I know her breasts are rising and her legs are getting thick
Her fingernails are polished
She's filling out so quick...
She wants to be a woman, but it's nowhere near her time
To force her in that direction is a malicious act of crime...
Don't touch her innocent beauty for she's a child of heavens' sky
Don't steal her from her mother's nest before she's strong enough to fly...
From the rib of a man she was made and from his seed conceived
to be protected and covered as the weaker vessel -
A godly man who is Jesus believes...
But the lust of your flesh held you captive
You would not call out to the Lord
You refused to put on the armor that held your eternal reward...
So, you'll go to hell a screaming
Her mind and body God will heal

You were used by the enemy to kill, destroy and steal...
But God got the glory
You can't get away with anything
He's her Master and her Savior
Her true and living King...

Pressing On

Pushing, pushing up a hill
A baby stroller, forgot the pill...
The winter air upon my face
I bundle my baby and quicken my pace...
No one to help me carry my load
So alone I travel a teen motherhood road...
The Daddy?
"I don't know where he's at."
He stopped coming around when my stomach got fat...
I hear he has a new girl now
Thinner, taller, medium brown...
My self-esteem is kinda low
Why didn't I listen? I shoulda said No!...
Pushing, pushing up a hill
A baby stroller, no condom, no pill…
I can't give up! Will not look back
No handouts here. No dope. No crack...
Must keep on pushing until I reach the top
Mistakes will never make me stop...
From the lowest valley to the highest hill
I'll press forward in God's mercy, grace, and will...

Philippians 3:14:
"I press towards the mark for the prize of the high calling of God in Christ Jesus"

Mourning to Morning

I cried relentlessly. I couldn't stop. I didn't want to stop. It was my right, my sorrow and no one had the right to tell me to calm down or to hush me up. Don't pat me on my back! Don't bring me any tissue! Just let the tears and snot run down my face and clothes.

No! I don't want to hear about God. What does He have to do with this? I called on Him. Yeah, I called on God. Maybe He just answers you. Maybe I should be mad at you and not Him. Maybe you didn't pray hard enough for me because if you did, 1 wouldn't be going through this pain.

What? I don't want to hear that same cliché about "weeping may endure for a night but joy cometh in the morning." Do you know how stupid you sound? What are you going to say next? "God don't make no mistakes." Well, He sure made one when He sent you to talk to me. Can you just shut up and leave me alone? It's obvious that you've never experienced what I am going through.

I'm sorry. Please forgive me. Thank you for trying to help, but I must seek God on my own for "a peace that passes all understanding."

Oh God! Why did you allow this to happen to me? I thought that you loved me? I go to church. I pray and read my Bible. You said that "goodness and mercy shall follow me all the days of my life." Ain't nothing good and merciful about this situation. I feel like your servant Job being persecuted for nothing. God, did you give Satan permission to attack me? If you did, I want to thank you for having so much confidence in me, but I would like to have your hedge of protection placed back around me please. You see, God, I can't do anything without you. For you are the Rock of My Salvation; My Hiding Place; My Shield and Buckler.

God, how long will this process take? You know, this mourning thing. It's a drag. My stomach feels funny. I don't want to see the light of day. I'd rather be alone. No words seem soothing. Pain embraces and holds my soul in captivity. My spirit feels heavy. When will this cloud lift? Will I ever make sense of this? I wish this day had never come. The inevitable is here. The thing that I most feared has found a place in me. Now I must see, feel, and taste what the first man, Adam, cursed me with – death. I can't run and hide from it. There are no animal skins that I can cover myself with to keep from being naked in the face of this trial and tribulation. I must stand before you God and allow you to take me through the process of becoming whole once again.

This thing has changed me. Life has taken on a brand new meaning for me. Days and nights are different. My approach to life is more definite and precise. I'm beginning to think things through. Everything isn't as funny as I use to think. I'm more focused now. I hear more and see more than I ever did before. I'm more sensitive to my surroundings. God's word is starting to make more sense to me. I feel like I'm standing on the brink of a brand new day. Nothing is the same anymore. There are different roads to travel, higher hills to climb, deeper depths to go, and yes, even more tears to cry.

Life has proven to me, more now than ever, that our seasons are many and we must be anchored in Christ if our trials and tribulations are going to redefine and refine our faith in Him.

I've gone from 'Mourning to Morning.'

"Blessed are they that mourn: for they shall be comforted." (Matthew 5:4)

God is Love

1 John 4:8

"Falling in love with God is the greatest romance
To seek Him is the greatest of all adventures
To find Him is the greatest human achievement"

Author Unknown

Falling in Love with God

> "Falling in love with God is the greatest of all romances; to seek Him is the greatest of all adventures; to find Him is the greatest human achievement." – Author Unknown

Some women have chosen to fall in love with a man before knowing the love of Jesus Christ. Her desperate cry for love, companionship, protection, and security has caused her to say "I do" to emotions, needs, and, wants that could have been met by her Savior if she had only fallen in love with Him first.

Now bound to a relationship that is not grounded in Christ or ordained by Him, she finds herself still empty and searching for fulfillment of her emotions, needs and wants. This feeling of emptiness causes her to hate the day that she uttered her vows, "Till death do we part." And, death is just what parted them. Satan knows how powerful a godly man and woman are together so he crafted a plan to attack the man and woman in the Garden of Eden. A kingdom divided against itself cannot stand. Satan's motive is to divide and conquer the man and woman. Genesis 2:18 says, "Then the Lord God said, 'It is not good for the man to be alone; I will make him a helper suitable for him.'" This suitable helper was a woman. It was not another man. The marriage covenant that God instituted between the man and the woman is so powerful that it can bring down Satan's kingdom. He knew this union would expand God's Kingdom in the earth realm. Therefore, Satan set out to bring about its death.

Not seeking Jesus first gives Satan an advantage over your relationship, whether you are married or dating. The enemy comes in swiftly to kill, steal, and destroy whatever chances there might be for your relationship to be pleasing to God. Without a strong spiritual foundation in Christ, the enemy will eat away at the very fiber of your love for one another. Arguments lead to bitterness, lack of intimacy and infidelity resulting in the death of the relationship.

Sisters, when you put a man's intimacy before your intimacy with God, you violate His word which separates you from Him.. Exodus 20:3 says, Thou shall have no other gods before me." Don't make your man your god. Submit yourself wholeheartedly to the God of heaven and earth, and he will prepare a king for you.

God promises you the abundant life if you seek Him first. Romans 6:33 says, "But seek ye first the Kingdom of God and His all of his righteousness and all these things shall be added unto you." What things? God will bless you with things that will fill your desire for love, companionship, protection, and security.

Whatever you are in need of God will give it to you in due season. God created you. Therefore, He knows exactly what you need in a man.

So, don't go searching for a man. The word of God says, "He who finds a wife finds a good thing, and obtaineth favor from the Lord" (Proverbs 18:22). You see, God's man is supposed to find you. When you are about your Father's business, He will surely take care of your business. The longer you are out of the presence of God, the longer it will take for your king to find you. Simply going to church will not do. You must Fall in love with God! He desires a relationship with you.

Sisters, separate yourself from those people, places, and things that keep you out of the presence of God. Stop playing silly boyfriend/girlfriend games. Get right with God. You do not want to be yoked up with the wrong person the rest of your life. That's bondage. Why put yourself or someone else in that situation. Be truthful in your relationships.

My sisters, Jesus Christ came to set the captives free. Be set free by Falling In Love with God; it is the greatest of all romances; seek Him; it is the greatest of all adventures; and I hope you find Him because it is the greatest human achievement.

"Make Love to Me, God"

Make love to me God. Blow gently on my skin...
Make love to me God. Touch my body dwell within...
Wrap your arms around me. I want to nuzzle in your breast...
I have need for your refuge. My mind and body I must rest...
I know that I'm a big girl. You've given me many years...
No more cuddling like a baby. No one to comfort my weary tears...
I thirst for the softness of your spirit and the warmth of your embrace...
Kiss my forehead. Hold me close. Let your hands caress my face...
My outer shell may seem tough and my words full and strong...
But my inner man burns with desire, for my soul to you belong...
As you kiss my body heavenly, sweet tears roll from my eyes...
My body lying motionless; in precious moments my spirit cries...
Make love to me God. I'm your woman, a big girl, a baby in need...
Make love to me God. My spirit man and soul for you doth bleed...

Psalms 116:1-2

I love the Lord, because he hath heard my voice and my supplications. Because he hath inclined his ear unto me, therefore will I call upon him as long as I live.

Women

Women be sittin around talkin bout
Hurt, and pain, and midnight rain...
Don't want no man no more
Hit the door cause he be poor for sure...
No money, no honey, no slickin and sliddin
No rump roast riding...
Women be laughin crazy and waving hands lazy
Itching and twitching, b-itching, bewitching
"Girl, he be trippin all the time."
Well, you know what I say
No Money, No Honey

Women be sitting around talkin bout
Hurt, and pain, and midnight rain...
Hurt, and pain, and midnight rain...

Taking the Blame

Go ahead. Admit it.

You don't have the problem. It's the other person.

Go ahead. Point the finger. He made you do it. He is the blame.

If it wasn't for him, you'd be all right.

How foolish you were to let him play you like a fool. You didn't do nothing wrong.

It was his fault, right?

Well. Wait a minute. Let's rewind the tape.

Let's re-examine the facts.

Now you say that you were sitting at the table reading your Bible when he walked over to you and said, "Is this seat taken?" You looked up, smiled, and said, "No." Six months later you were pregnant?

This is one of those times you should have said, yes, this seat is taken.

The enemy came upon you like a thief and left you empty.

He broke in, got what he wanted and made his exit through the back door, leaving you wide open for more satanic attacks. He took all your honey and your money. You thought you could change him. Didn't you?

When the devil took up residency in your life, he filled a void that you didn't let God fill . The enemy smelled your vulnerability.

He hugged you. He caressed you. He told you that you were beautiful, smart, and wonderful. You were the only person in his life to ever make him feel like a man. How understanding you were.

You dressed him up like a king. You told him that everything was going to be all right and not to be so hard on himself. You cooked him meals fit for a king and even helped him pay his bills down to his child support payments just so he wouldn't go to jail.

You thought just reading the Bible would shield you from attacks?

It's doing the Bible that covers us and wards off those fiery darts that the enemy hurls at us.

So you see? It's no time to be playing the blame game.

As long as you make accusations, the enemy will continue to conquer you. You must assume the responsibility for your own actions.

I know that you are hurt and bitter. You didn't know that you were opening yourself up to be belittled and shamed. Your intentions were good.

Now let's focus on righteous intentions. They bring joy to your heavenly father and keeps you covered by the Blood of the Lamb giving you spiritual discernment.

Come on let's pray and ask God for forgiveness and guidance. You're going to need a lot of prayer for your new baby.

Keep this scripture in your heart:

> Matthew 6:33
> "But, seek ye first the Kingdom of God and all of His righteousness and all these things shall be added unto you."

Hold Out for a Praying Brother

A brother who can't pray for you can't fight demons for you. I'm talking about spiritual warfare. You need help with stuff that gets deep down in your bones and visit you in your dreams.

Let me make this thing plain; Demons will attack you in the midnight hour while you're fast asleep right next to your man. The only way that he can discern that you're under physical attack in the spirit realm is if he has a strong prayer life with you. Praying together on a daily basis connects you together in the spirit. The Bible says: "For where two or three are gathered in my name, there I am in the midst of them" (Matthew 18:3). Women, you must not only be physically attracted to a man but spiritually attracted as well.

Satan is like the movie character "Freddie Kruger." "He's coming to get you." He is like a roaring lion seeking whom he may devour. He likes to attack you while you are asleep. He does not fight fair. He comes at you when he thinks you are defenseless and when your guards are down. If you must have a man, make sure that you have a god-fearing man attached to you spiritually to assist you in warding off spiritual attacks. The word of God says "one can chase a thousand and two can put ten thousand to flight." You need to be spiritually armed. When Satan shows up, he comes with a legion of demons. You and your man must be prepared for spiritual warfare.

One night in the cradle of my sleep I was sexually attacked by a demonic spirit. I tried to fight off the attack. I struggled with all of my might. Demons have supernatural strength. Humans are no match for them physically. I began pleading the "Blood of Jesus Christ." In my call for help, Jesus delivered me from my spiritual attack. As I returned to a physically conscious state, I could feel the pressure on my inner thighs that was applied by the demon in its attempt to force itself upon me. I felt violated. All I could do was curl up in a fetal position and whimper like a wounded animal. My mind started wondering; "Will anybody believe this actually happened to me? " How could this be? I was doing everything that I could to serve God. I wasn't a carnal-minded Christian. I didn't play church. I was seeking God with all my heart. I was constantly asking God to "search me, know me and try me to see if there be any wicked way in me and lead me in the way everlasting" (Psalms 139:23-24).

Suddenly it dawned on me. This attack was an attempt by Satan to destroy the confident and faithful woman I had become in Jesus Christ name. Satan wanted to put fear in me so that I would shut my mouth and not proclaim the good news of the Gospel. I quickly repositioned my thinking. I leaped to my feet and started praying like a warrior rebuking the attack.

I started preaching and teaching vehemently from pulpits and any other platform that I was graced with about Satan's vicious attacks to keep God's people powerless and afraid of operating in authority. I relentlessly admonished people to surround themselves with powerful and anointed people that operated in the authority of Jesus Christ. Right now, I am telling you to do the same thing. You don't need any kind of man, you need a god-fearing man. And just because he's in the pulpit doesn't make him God's choice for you.

Sisters, never look at a man or desire him based on his outward beauty or earthly treasures. They are only temporary pleasures. But set your affections on things above where Christ sits at the right hand of the father (Colossians 3:1-5). And remember, don't go after a man. God said that "when a man finds a wife, he finds a good thing." Therefore, stop your searching. If you prepare yourself for Christ, He will prepare a husband for you.

And by all means, let the brother get his stuff in order before putting your life in his life. Trying to fix him up, pay for his stuff, cook for him and please him sexually while he's still struggling trying to make ends meet will only frustrate you once the novelty of sex has worn off. It is not your job to be his mother.

Let him get out of jail (if that's the case); deal with the baby mama drama and child support; get a clean bill of health; clean up his credit report; get his own place and keep it clean and paid for; seek a home church and be a member in good standing for at least a year. And, he must learn to pray for you, others, and himself in Jesus' name. This is just to mention a few things that you need to let him do on his own.

God supplied Adam with all provisions before He gave him a wife (Genesis 2). Let God equip the man spiritually and naturally before you violate your destiny with your untamed flesh. The Bible teaches that "if we walk in the spirit we will not gratify the lust of the flesh (Galatians 5:16). If you are already married or think this man will be your husband one day, be a virtuous woman. Let him see Christ in you (Proverbs 31).

Women are naturally caregivers. While he's getting himself together, give yourself to Christ wholeheartedly. In doing so, He will direct you into greener pastures in relationships. God called a man to be the head of the home. If women keep picking men up and brushing them off, they become weak and dependent. In short, they become "mama boys." Congratulations, you've helped create a spoiled monster. You've helped Satan decapitate him and de-throne him when God called him to be a king.

In conclusion, sister, you must ask God to keep you. He desires to prepare a godly man for you that has the power and authority in Jesus' name to help you progress through your seasons. If you have children, you better hold out for a praying man. Who and what attacks you spiritually and naturally have crafted a plan to sift your children as wheat so they can't operate in their God-given ability. The last thing you want to do is introduce a carnal-minded, unsaved man into the presence of your being who can't discern Satan's attacks in your life or in his own life. His lack of interest for the spiritual things of God will plant seeds that will take root and grow and devour all that you are (children, health, wealth, and emotional and spiritual being).
Sisters, Please ***Hold Out for a Praying Brother***!

"I Praise Thee Because
I am Fearfully and
Wonderfully made..."

Psalm 139:14

A Declaration to Me

I refuse to treat you like you treat me.
I am determined to be the better person.
Although your words and actions are hurtful and malicious,
I am still determined to be the better person.
I will not let my hurts, habits or hang-ups decapitate you or bound you.
I will not let your hurts, habits and hang-ups decapitate me or bound me.
I now know who I am in Christ; my body, my soul and my spirit are free.

Madam C.J. Walker

Thanks Madam C.J. for the hair
Your beauty products make Black women
beautiful every where
We can wear our hair in curls,
In a bush or in braids
Thanks to your mixture of beauty aids

My Hair

My Hair is who I am
So don't be looking, shaking, taking and swearing
That's right!
I 'Double D Dare' you to return to the hair
That once described us as being the royalty of the
'Mother Land'
Sweating and struggling to remain unbound
Free from oppression, depression, obsession
From changes that claim us to tame us to name us
That's right
My Hair is who I am
Kinky, twisted, shifted, lifted
Making a statement, Denial of hate
Scent of my Tribal Ancestry
I'm straight!

African Beauties

From the Huts of Africa, From the River Nile
From the South to the North Stolen Miles and Smiles...
Great Queens Great Scenes
Great Tribes Great Cries
Dancing to their beat, Praising with their feet
Earthly soil from the Mother Land
Defying death's defeat...
Bearing souls of generations deep within her womb
Standing strong in the struggle, A nation's plotted doom...
Black as the night; Tan as sand
She carries the pain. She carries the dream
Lifted voice
Echoing Herstory's Scream...
Rising from life's deepest despair
Embracing her beauty, Beholding what's rare...
Exposing the chosen; Revealing Satan's stealing Crushing slavery's lie
Refusing to die...
Determination for a nation's Preservation, Predestination
Reaching, teaching, preaching, faith in Salvation
From the Huts of Africa. From the River Nile
From the South to the North
Stolen Miles and Smiles
Great Queens
Great Scenes
Great Tribes
Great Cries
Dancing to their heat
Praising with their feet
Earthly soil from the Mother Land
Defying death's defeat...

Vagina Madness

Womanhood, Motherhood
Creation between her thighs
She's been through some trauma
And had some sad good-byes
There was Mike and Kenny
And some guy she didn't quite know
There was Rachel and Trina
An experiment that didn't grow
On days when she goes to the doctor
She's propped and spread real wide
Here comes the clamp; watch out, girl
There goes her joy and pride
One time she got a crazy idea
With a razor, she cut all her hair
All the itching and the scratching
Left her in great despair
When she cycles through her days
The journey can be tough
The cramping and the bloating
The padding's not enough
She enjoys all her seasons
In spring she's frisky, untamed
Summer has her attention
Enough with this childhood game
Autumn can be unpredictable
She fights the fear of age
Can she stand up to the pressure
During this menopausal rage?
Winter is a settling time
She cruises through her golden days
Finding pleasure in her accomplishments
No longer led by vagina's old ways

Vagina Madness; you say that's crazy
You've never heard of such a wild thing
Put your hand between your legs
Keep it there until you get a wedding ring
Well, pardon my expression, honey
But I'm not trying to sound cute
The womb between your legs
It is the bearer of good fruit
Your little sister and brother
Your mama and daddy too
Had to come pass the Vagina
Pushing and pulling brought them through
This Fertile Crescent Oasis
A creation formed from above
Should never lose its power
It's God way of spreading his love
Rape and molestation
Cancer and other disease
Robs her of her blessings
Producing barren seeds
That's why it's Vagina Madness
You gotta fight to protect this, girl!
The enemy wants to destroy her
To keep kings and queens from entering this world
Affirm that you love your Vagina!
Your woman-motherhood
Be so proud to know her
Vagina Madness is S0000 good!

Bridging Beautiful Black Women

Beautiful Black women with multi-colored skin
Tan, chocolate, bubbling brown You're a queenly African...
Beautiful Black Women with curly, braided, silky hair
You are an earthly vessel of treasure made for tender loving care
Your virtuousness is attractive, a vision to behold
Strong and dignified you are more precious than silver and gold
Admire your African sisters Embrace them for who they are
Mothers, sisters, daughters Those near and from afar
It's time we come together
Bridge the gap that keeps us apart
It's time we come together so true sisterhood can start
Now, the devil deceived Mother Eve
Out of the garden lost in sin
No sisters to surround her
Thorns and thistles to begin
Be your sister's keeper
Bear the burdens that come her way
Rejoice in her blessings
Intercede for her when you pray
It's time we bridge together
A circle of unity and love
Hold her hand. She is special
A spiritual gift from above

*"And He put a new
song in my mouth,
even praise unto our
God: many shall see it
and fear, and shall
trust in the Lord."*

Psalm 40:3

I Wanna Be Where You Are...

(Rap Song)

Chorus
I wanna be where you are, Lord
I wanna be where you are, Lord
I wanna be where you are, Lord
I wanna be where you are, Lord
Women of distinction you look so fine everywhere you go you got Jesus on your mind...
Trials and tribulations hit you night and day
But you bow to King Jesus cause he's the only way...
Georgie Porgie Puddin and Pie
He kissed you girl and he made you cry...
Thought you have a man but you had a boy tried to strip you of all your pride and joy...
But you looked to the Savior to help you cope Now you got your Holy Ghost Hope...
You got a call on your life to preach the word
But the devil keeps saying, "Women shouldn't be heard, Women shouldn't be heard, Women shouldn't be heard"…
But Jesus says, I know you got fear
But come up a Little Higher and let me whisper in your ear...
Power, love and a sound mind that's your name
The world, Satan and your flesh don't have no claim...
So you stir up the gift deep inside and give God all the Glory He's Jehovah EL-Shadi…

Angels Over Me

You clapped your hands
You flapped your wings
You blew your breath
And your angels sing
To lift me up from life's
despair because you love me and you care
You clapped your hands
You flapped your wings
You blew your breath
And your angels sing
I stand in awe of your majestic grace
I live to see your glorious face